THE ODYSSEY SINGER

The Odyssey Singer

Michael Conway

FLOATING ISLAND PUBLICATIONS
POINT REYES STATION

Published by:
Floating Island Publications
P.O. Box 516
Point Reyes Station, California 94956

ISBN: 0-912449-17-9

The author wishes to thank Ann Wigfield and Elizabeth Ptak for their help with the illustrations in this book, and especially Gene Ptak for his generous kindness and support.

CONTENTS

The Odyssey Singer

A Poem for Dancing

Between the Shouting and the Toad

The Odyssey Singer

Athene

Gray-eyed the goddess Athene
comes when the plot needs a turn,
silently showing her wisdom,
leaving before it is known.

Dimly from out of the shadows
she enters the scene from the rear,
watches the ongoing action,
waits for her cue to appear.

Most wise the man who can listen
without his critical mind
finding when she has vanished
what she has left him to find.

Sometimes the goddess Athene
takes the part of the fool,
leaves what passes for wisdom
but is not wisdom at all.

Wise is the man who will know when
she plays this opposite game;
will turn his back on his insight,
continuing on with the scene.

Sometimes the goddess Athene
comes like a cry in the night
piercing the dream of the sleeper
before it can sink from his sight;

in shadows there at his bedside
she watches him try to recall,
speaks the one word he searches,
flys away like an owl.

Invoking her guidance for one thing
sometimes she leaves you instead
a piece of another puzzle
long put out of your head.

Sometimes she seems to leave nothing
passing invisibly through;
but something is subtly shifted
and all the long known is now new.

The brow of the goddess Athene
encompassing space and time
projects for the favored who hear her
into the serial mind

and there her luminous solutions,
dimensioned from beyond the beyond,
she simplifies to stage props
for the play to move on and around.

So all hail the goddess Athene,
she who continues to come
after all other gods have deserted!
I offer her, grateful, these poems.

Calypso

Sea nymph Calypso
where have I been
waking to find myself
floating in your charms?

You have been with me forever.
No, there was once a time before.
You have never left my arms.

Calypso Sea Nymph
there are pearls in your hair.
They pull it down across your shoulders.
I preferred your shoulders bare.

I have always worn my hair thus.
No, once it flowed out in the water.
I have always had them there.

Calypso Calypso
call your father.
Tell him you should set me free.
Give me back my next tomorrow.

No, Poseidon is a tempest god.
He will listen to you if you ask him.
He will only roil the water.

Circe

Patroness of women I
keep my lovers in a sty;
men are little less than hogs
though they swagger like the gods.

Come and taste my potion love;
fatten on the joys it gives.
Be content to root and swill
keeping mind but losing will.

Spider, spider, weave a web.
Silken sheets spread my soft bed.
Midnight hero, at the dawn
be not woman, be not man.

Once that I was mad for magic,
moonshapes woven through the mind
came to me a brow all sunlit
filled to truth with all it finds.

Comes to me a sun bright hero,
a man who wills to turn my world,
who speaks to the gods and to the rainbow,
and shows me how love can unfold.

Oh! Love, if beauty you will have
for his expanding soul to sing,
beauty, all I have, I give,
though left alone I wither young.

He Sings to Circe

I.

The seed will sprout, the green will grow
without a living sacrifice;
there is no need for blood to flow
to keep this changing world in place.

Your magic moods may soothe the winds
and turn the tide when time is ripe,
but I can transmute elements
and hold the sunset golden bright;

There is no magic that can dim
the constancy of light;
the eye clouds over but the sun
has never seen the night.

II.

Man is a fickle thing, a heedless climber
        searching a way to get beyond mankind;
but woman is not and she must cover—
        protective the womb that keeps the seed with time.

If she deny, soon there'll be no denying.
        But he can dare deny even the stars
and searching higher, lower reach a striving
        that she, redundant to the earth, abhors.

He Sings to the Trojan Boy

I.

What did you sing to Circe?
My lust for her.
What else did you sing?
I sang songs of stars. My lust for them.
Sing a song of me, for me.
All my songs are songs of you, for you.
Yes; but sing one openly.
Sing a song so all will know.

II.

Come to me my cocky boy.
Our love is more than song.
Each in the other's arms made one,
molded one to clay,
let's throw our love upon a wheel
and kick it to the speed
that skillful potters need
and with our fingers pull it up.
And turn and turning on the wheel
and pull it gently, roughly up
and turn and turning on the wheel
spread it out into a cup.
And turn and turning on the wheel
blossom it into a vase
of classic line and classic grace
turning and turning on the wheel
where golden figures play:

boxing, wrestling, in the race
for the careless laurel crown
to frame a face
a brow, a line of nose and chin,
a flowing cheek,
a cupid bow of lip
a mouth held straight.
And eyes
deep pools
that deep within
hold the silent mystery
of see and seen.
Each in the other's arms made one
holding in the ecstasy
that only man with man can know
turn and turning on the wheel
holding in the ecstasy
until the night is done
such love cannot be sung.

He Sleeps Alone

Alone, alone dark in his doubt,
but much too strong to weep
the hero spreads his blanket out
and crawls into his sleep.

Alone, alone he sleeps alone;
and lonely is his dream—
and sometimes tossing he will moan—
and waking sometimes scream.

Remembering His Dream

I've heard the melody the ancient truth
has always played upon the thighs of youth;
I know that love transcends impotent stones
transmuting granite boulders into bones,
that fire will find new flesh as flesh grows old
and that humanity cannot go cold.

But what I know is now a quiet zone
where mortal tendrils freeze and all lose hold.

Odysseus to the World

I would have no man lightly know
 the weakness I succeed:
I am the gathering of the brow,
 the conquest and the deed.

I don't deny that I have done
 some things that make me cringe
when I am in my room alone.
 What man tames all his sins?

Nor to deny the flesh of life:
 I live with many scars
and many times I fail in strength;
 yet I live toward the stars.

Song

The world is mine to sing
and oh! the joy I sing today
tomorrow though it pass away
for hate, for war, for petty things
that people do or say
I cannot lose today.
I cannot weep, I cannot weep
though hate and war rage on.
The breath comes in too strong.
And circling full around the heart
must leave again in song.

Dodona

Fluttering leafy faces
With tongues that never lie
People the magic places
Where acorns come to tree
And all they speak is one long sigh
Of days as green as these gone by
And greener prophesy.

Fluttering leafy faces,
Dodona, bred of thee
Shine in the gnarled spaces
That arch the temple sky
And through the noon of this green lea
Their laughing tongues foretell a tree
Where no tongues prophesy.

Elpenor

Shadow thin
Elpenor
passes in
through a door
not there before
then
closing
that is no more.

Odysseus to the Navigator

If you must chart the ocean surface
by an island here and there,
beware the winds that cross your purpose
blowing you off course too far
beyond an island or a star.
The more that you throw out your anchor,
the more you lose all hope of port.
The winds that scatter bring again together;
the winds that gather blow again apart.

Penelope

Shuttle in and shuttle through
shuttle out and in again,
cribs of flax and wool
woman soft and fine
tightening to her pull
over polished fingers
fill the warp of time.

But the sun is such a fool:
on the loom the Odyssey
ravels undefined,
for by night by moonlight
she and all the slave girls
work with flashing fingers
unspinning clouds of twine.

And as deftly as she wove it
do the women claim the war
every part of every battle
the entire heroic weft
back around the spools
fluffed into the cribs,
all becomes what was before.

All those days of fetlock fury!
All that tapestry of travels!
All they raise is clouds of lint
leaving but the trace
thin upon the lintels
of the war for Helen's face,
of his ranging Odyssey.

What the sun achieves by day
moonlight fingers rip away
and the true Penelope,
wishing that her fingers would
weave the wandering sailor home,
weeps that she must always be
weaving what she must destroy.

Odysseus Lost at Sea

I feel your fingers yet upon the loom;
this very moment you have shot the shuttle through,
but all direction gone and far from home
I cannot hope to come again to you.
  I am an old man huddled in the dawn
  and have, dear wife, been from old friends too long.

When wounds were hot and new they had a throb,
a glow that gave me courage to any deed;
but now the war is won, the scars are numb,
the flesh, the friends I fought with, all are dead;
  and longing to be one with what is gone
  I am an old man huddled in the dawn.

My seed is sown and given to my son.
My body rattles down, wasted with the winds.
For what I know my voyage now is done;
I drown today—and gone are all good friends!
  But do not weep. Here huddled in the dawn
  I am an old man waiting to be born.

Three Songs to the Sun

I.

Time has a way of folding inward when the sun
touches its flower, and hardening to seed.
Yesterday, a million yesterdays are one
when darkness comes and I fold into sleep.

When morning comes the unfolding starts again:
forever outward from what went before.
I wake to find that darkness was a dream
and now the sun is shining on the flower.

II.

The sun is not a god.
Although his strength elates me
I do not worship him
the way I used to do:
Reason dissects his light.
Yet day rolls into night
and even in the search for gods
the sun must be served.

III.

The sun is the god of now.
What I have been he cancels out.
What I will be he laughs at.
What I am now he shines upon
and fills with warmth and song.

So much to do, so much to do.
So many songs to finish.
I cannot face the sunset now
with any peace of mind.

He Comes Again to a Garden

This garden has been with me
a jewel in my mind
through many dusty battles,
through many days at sea,
through many nights of labored love,
the cold expanse of been and done.
Time was and time will be.
Time was and time will be.

Now with it here around me
it seems I was returning
however wide I traveled
to the here now around me
and the now now here,
always was returning
to this jewel box garden.
Time was and time will be.
Time was and time will be.

Always was returning,
to this here and now of time,
to this intricate space around me,
to the coruscating garden
green and red and diamond,
silver, gold and blue,
to this sun-filled garden.
Time was and time will be.
Time was and time will be.

Time now and I wander the pathways,
come to each hidden corner,
each turn of bed and tree,
each sunlight into shadow.
I hold my breath that maybe
a new gate will be there
under jewel and vine,
over moss and stone.
A new gate will be there
and through it another garden
leading out of time,
leading out of time.

He Comes to Another Time

Here is a garden opening before me
reflecting backwards into time before.
In both directions stretching on forever
leafy shadow faces call me on.

Penelope long weaving at the loom,
Telemachus, tall son to carry on,
Circe and the Trojan boy to sing to.
What have they to do with cars and airplanes?
With rockets sending sons up to the moon?
Are they from seed I left for him to carry?

Was it through a garden gate or a mirror?
Was I really part of that once time before?

I remember walking through a garden
different from this now and yet the same:
shadows prophesying all around me,
telling me there was a hidden door.

Here I sit and write with a computer,
order my daily life with microwaves,
have dials that tune to bring in old ones singing:
Wolfgang, Johann, Domenico, Orphee,
an unknown singer on an unknown shore.
Telemachus, my son and now my father.

Was I really part of that once time before?
Was it through a garden gate or a mirror?

The Odyssey Singer

The loom is now a computer;
the singer, the always same.
Around and around without meaning
a spindle of words in his brain
like Penelope weaving her wool
into the warp of time
scrolling backwards and forwards the shuttle
upwards and downwards the screen
meaning slowly but steadily filling
the warp of rhythm and rhyme.

Why does the Odyssey Singer
sing songs that have been sung before?
Weaving a piece of a puzzle
caught in a spinning of words
thus driven there is no why.
Back and forth with the shuttle
tightening sense and phrase
digging through glittering nonsense
fragmented pottery pieces
coins that have purchased a slave
a harp that is nothing but backbone
covered by dust that was tapestry
hung on the wall of a grave.

The slave is now a computer
a stove and a washing machine
and music from every dimension
surrounds him as microwaves.
Why does the Odyssey Singer
sit and stare at the screen
hoping for patterns to take him
back to another age?
Why do the archeologists
catalog grave after grave?
He sings but a fragment of textile,
a patch for a tapestry lost;
but a part of an ancient story
and hooked to a telling of stars.

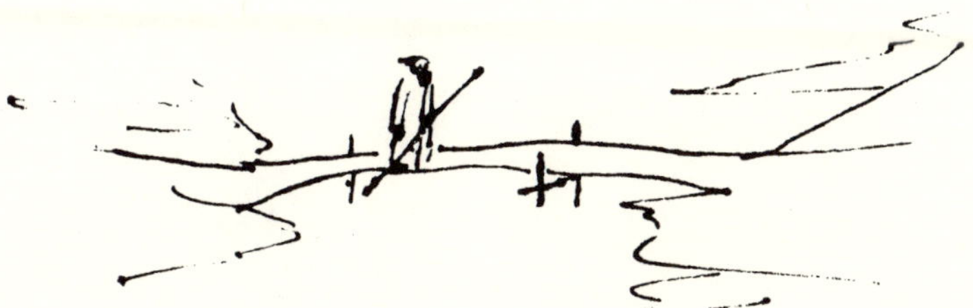

Twilight

Long into the twilight I have dreamed:
to the darkness I have slowly come
and with me brought about me all un-named
a silent poem still luminous with the sun.

Though now the night is dark and deep around me,
though there is no defense against this dark
and shadows threaten inward like an army
I have its voiceless words about my heart.

And there they orbit in such subtle rhymes,
such subtle rhythms, with such grace,
reflecting wordless in the way of dreams
perfection fallen suddenly to place.

The greatest poem is utter quiet, silence,
a heart that wreaths itself in silent chords,
a glow of unknown melodies and harmonies:
a dream truth known by rhyme and not by words.

But, for still the dark keeps pushing in,
dreams cannot be remembered without words.
The poem is the poet whether he sing
songs of substance, only flickering thoughts—

songs of deception, songs of naked honesty,
whether his be a true or a bubble odyssey.

Morning Light

Morning light is a golden ring,
a promise kept of a fairy king,
a gift returned for a changeling boy
much loved by him by star, by moon.

Tall in a shroud a figure stands
invisible to daylight eyes
offering a jeweled horizon,
fading fast lingering on.

Day now becomes a petty thing
unless you strive to keep that ring.
So weave a poem. Weave it thrice.
And weave it through with threads of night,

left and right across the brain,
science woven through with rhyme,
part-was leavings of the mind,
things you thought to leave behind.

For things stand sharpest when they're seen
against the darkness of a dream.
Science can analyze the day;
art must show what fades away.

So many painters speak of light:
old masters placing specks of white;
thus morning teaches us to see
by placing sunlight in a tree.

Morning Music

Play Bach the prelude number one;
let the morning sun shine on a rose;
feed the ribbon time between your fingers;
be the instant world as it unfolds.

In the instant now of this unfolding
feel your fingers shifting with the chords
playing out an endless morning of roses—
playing Bach the prelude number one.

Light at Noon

Light at noon is a diamond.
All that is is seen.
Every particle of science
reflects from spin and dart and bounce,
reflects to fields of green.

Light at noon is a diamond.
Nature is hard and clear.
Every sun reflecting leaf
with deeper green and black beneath
is outlined by bright air.

Light at noon is a diamond.
The sky burns blue and white.
Every movement of the breeze
throws prism colors through the trees
bedazzling the eye.

Afternoon Light

The window forces light where gulls suspend
to take the shape of her pale thighs
and fuses the tight patterns in the room
into white space time wide where she too flies.

The clock is stopped. The rug spreads on the floor.
Even her rounded breasts flatten
in these dimensions. She is so bright! More
than a girl sunning in an object room.

The light is smooth against the flesh and still
and cold and going slantwise; and
the dark sea rolls beyond the second hill
and she is here, carved from the flight of gulls.

Starlight

Filaments of pinpoint light
spin out across the waves of night
and weave a sky.

Stitching, stitching space to time
science is a nursery rhyme
to know the stars.

Eyes the size of universe
look deep into themselves and see
the start of time.

Seeing then becomes an end
and looking out a start and then
starts all again.

Adventuring through time and stars
a space ship thrusting through the mind
lands on the lawn.

The starflowers look and see it there;
the night moths flicker in the air
around its door.

Ribbons of time and star spun space
spiral until they coincide
within their eyes.

The smallest particle of physics,
the greatest sphere of universe,
all coincide.

Infinities click into place
and every star there shining gives
sights out of time.

Time weary at last the traveler
looks back at what has gone before
and then goes on.

The starflowers watch all through the night
to see the traveler in his flight
on into time.

Mother Goose and William Blake
will rise, and constellations make
next time around.

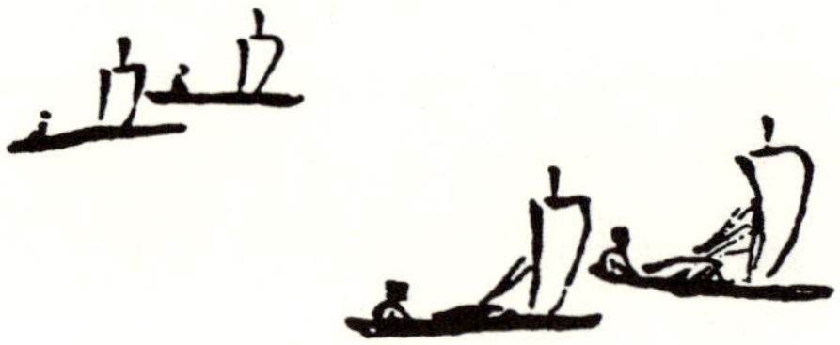

What the Traveler Saw

Time is equal time plus one
across the universe
and measuring the furthest star
time distance to and fro
and probing infinitely small
space pointed toward a naught:
Science soon will know it all
and then . . . Then what?

The boy that Michelangelo
took flesh and turned to stone
has leapt down from his pedestal
and come into the room.
The universe of art and song
we measure eye and ear;
but time plus one good talk must end
and then . . . What then?

Calypso swimming through the mind
reaches to hold you down;
so stand art on its pedestal,
store science in its books:
new odysseys will take their thrust
from being what has been,
burning it all till time plus one
and then . . . And then!

Time is equal time plus one
across the universe
and . . .

The Traveler on the Mount of Gods

Now comes the traveler to a mountain stream,
a foam of brush strokes on a long silk scroll,
a thrust of mountain lost in veils of mist:
overhanging crags and caves, towers of rock and cloud.

Somewhere in the mist a summit looms
more left than right, but drifting now and then.

Around a turn of trail a waterfall
pours waves of sound into a steep ravine,
white swirling sound through which he climbs.
The silk unrolls. Another landscape fills the brain.

Above the tumult there are high plateaus,
regions of space where holy roosters crow.

And through these regions now the faceless gods
wander back and through, wander in and out;
encounter them and look, they disappear;
ignore, they whisper shadows in your ear.

Unwinding art from dream and dream from art
poet and painter weave the human heart.

So sight averted always right or left
he searches misty corners of his eyes;
he gathers shadows, floating shapes and rhymes,
flashing lights, oracles and prophecies.

Discharging circuits crackling through the brain:
lightning along the nerves discharging pain.

In time pain ends, the shadows take a form:
row upon row the godlike figures come
slow music eddying in their luminous wake:
the mind envelops all the cube of space.

The silk rerolls. But now through all the scene
the sound of falling waters is serene.

Scholarly travelers talk about a world
which waters and mists conceal beyond approach;
but poets endlessly sing these sacred mountains
floating through varying deepnesses of cloud.

Where east is mirror depths of mountain peaks,
blue upon blue, reflections of reflections.

Passing through the traveler sees it all:
the brush strokes and the misty mountain peak
the pines upon the rocks, the waterfall,
the fabric's texture and the lonely trail.

Where west is random blips upon a screen,
a silent ground of swirling background snow.

History Lesson

Even Yeats refused to know
the truth of Michelangelo.
Beneath the loving muscled stone,
beneath the veils they painted on
when such as he would never look
who can trust the history book?

Singers by the Sea

Coming now again to middle age,
home from what I was, richer in time,
richer in having been and am not now
I sort through piles of then and gone.

Filaments of music spider woven through the air
connecting time to time to time.

Limber body, stiff; pinpoint vision, blurred;
but still from inside looking out, the same;
and always hearing music, music, music:
and not so old not to be born again.

Everywhere I've been I've been before;
enigma variations on a theme.

Youth discovers, leaves life in a heap;
middle age stoops down to sort it out:
London bridges, golden sand, the river;
a maiden with a dulcimer, a man with a blue guitar.

Accomplished fingers strumming their instruments:
singers by the sea on another shore.

Time is a surf forever rolling in
then cresting on itself as it recedes:
bending down I sort and sort again
themes tossed up by waves from earlier seas.

Sorting, sorting trying to discover
the way I've come to get from there to here.

And not so young not to have traveled far,
not to have wandered up and down the river
searching from the mountain to the sea:
all brought home to scatter on the floor.

Sorting, sorting trying to discover
how seeds of then became this world of now.

Now again these searchings fill the brain.
And weaving them into sonata form,
beginning, middle, variation, end,
past and present come to harmony:

music spreading on and on and on
lapping against another singer's shore.

Children's Games

I.

Ten brave Greeks
inside a wooden horse.
    It was a squeeze.
    They did not sneeze.
And one jumped out.

II.

Achilles sulked inside his tent
to make the king of Greeks repent.
    How many days did he do it?
One two three four five six . . . heel!

III.

The horses raced across the field!
    The dust mixed with the blood!
The pain went screaming to the sky!
    And the gods looked on.

IV.

Zeus thunderer rages lightning
    the whole horizon round
and all the towers the Trojans built
    come tumbling to the ground.

The men are slain, the women raped,
    the children sold to slavers
and every child, each girl and boy,
    stands naked to their fingers.

V.

Homer came when it was done
and turned the war into a song.
But if they'd had the atom bomb
    what would he have sung?
Boom boom boom boom boom boom . . . gone!

Odysseus and the Sunset

At last Odysseus turns west toward the sun:
and wading from the shore on shivering knees
into the waves of freezing sunset seas
there suddenly his life comes all to one:
but spinning on, as it has always done,
the world that gave him flesh and mind and eyes
to see itself through him, O self disguise!
laughs round and round relishing the fun:

''Now all comes home! Now all. Yet still must seek.
O Brother Sunset, more.''—silence—''Me, speak,
and to one who personifies, Umph! True,
you've had your Mother Earth, your Father Sky,
your gods galore, but Brother Sunset, I,
indeed! Whammy, orange and green and blue—''

A Poem for Dancing
1960–1984

Prelude

—and then the dance,
the singing movement,
the silver sound of stars rimming the sky,
of atoms universing by,
the rhythm wide, and wide and high—

Round I

First you must bring her down to earth,
   There is no starting other,
The story must down here have birth,
   Stars are too high.

Then wake her from her silver trance,
   There is no starting other,
And set her spinning through the dance.
   Why? Don't ask why.

But keep her down upon the ground,
   There is no starting other,
For maidens dancing that first round
   Know how to fly.

And when she stops, then spin the world,
   There is no starting other,
Or all her flesh might be unfurled
   Into a sigh.

Stroke and stroke her limbs and brow,
   There is no starting other,
Make her feel that time is now,
   Not by and by.

Make her know, all flesh and bone,
   There is no starting other,
Her kinship is to sea and stone
   And not the sky.

Then give to her her mirror face,
   There is no starting other,
Her lonely smile must in this place
   Find some reply.

But set a bramble in her hair,
   There is no starting other,
She must not be unearthly fair
   To her own eye.

And though she yearns for flute and bell,
   There is no starting other,
Play your bassoons and drums as well
   Though she defy.

Tell and tell her tales of strife,
   There is no starting other,
Thus realize her into life
   And let her cry.

Let her weep, Oh she must weep,
   There is no starting other,
Let sorrows weigh her into sleep
   Till tears go dry.

But wake her if her dreams shine bright,
   There is no starting other,
She must fight serpents through this night
   And dread to die.

Interlude I

Each boulder, stone, each grain of sand
retumbled round with waves and rains
imposes on the measure of the dance.

Dull minerals, the rocks and clays,
with silent force spin to their place
and crystallize to honeycombs of dance.

Soft spoken cells fermenting down
reroot into more fertile sands
and blossom into passion flowers of dance.

With flesh the shapeless word responds,
and lifted into form by bones
steps out into the movement of the dance

and every movement is a phrase,
a muscle turned, a finger raised,
a hip sent rolling round to wilder dance.

Then as her foot presses the ground
to find the strength to dance the round
to find the rhyme and rhythm of the dance

then you are safe to let her go
for though she dances she won't know
the prophecy inherent in the dance.

Round II

Now must her story take its course;
Try not to interfere;
To meddle only makes things worse
and burdens you with care:
The stars have been forgotten.
The earth is all her cause.
Her vision is a spinning world
of rock and tree disguise,
of cups and bathtubs, sweets and sours,
breath and nails and dander.
All flashing with the nights and days
they dance and swirl around her.

Around, around the world spins
out in its space beyond;
but deep in the center flesh she is
set in a fairy land:
And there her once-upon-a-time—
though never less nor more,
though always on the same sad sea—
is on a clean, new shore
and for a time she is the queen
composing her new realm,
and for a time the oceans seem
tideless, almost calm.

(Ocean unto ocean,
on shores of space to time
the surf dimensions out a world
where all things have a name:
this and that, and there and when,
shoreline, sand and foam,
through and out, and up and down,
window, bed and room,

good and bad and rocking chair,
and vase of yellow flowers—
Ocean unto ocean,
tideless, almost calm.)

But soon the moon will fill her flesh—
you may not know just when—
and all around a higher surf
will break into her dreams.
Then she will wonder at the sea
as though not known before,
and wonder at the cresting waves
that break against the shore,
and wonder at the hairs that sprout
soft on the secret place.
She and the world that spins about
at last will come to phase.

Around, around she spins herself
until the world has stopped
and now, though silently out of breath,
she is at last grown up:
the cup is in the saucer
and all the rooms have walls:
geometry and algebra,
poetry, art and love,
lipstick, cars and sips of wine:
Try not to interfere;
To meddle only makes things worse
and burdens you with care.

(Ocean unto ocean
yet still the waves roll on
a wash of churning wishes
that surface in her dreams:
palaces and movie stars,
golden sands on other shores,
gardens once of paradise;
strong round arms to turn her round;
mouth and nose and brow and eyes;
tall ships on far horizons coming home.
Ocean unto ocean
churning on and on.)

Finally the wish that washes her
will suddenly take a name.
Billy will come, her new found lover—
so different, so the same.
And he'll take her breasts in his cupped hands
and drawing near kiss her,
and push himself in through the bands
of her tight hair
and lose what of him is alone
and fuse all out to in:
"O Mother, I have come back home;
leaving was the only sin."

Interlude II

Mother, the children in you
struck from the ancestor flesh,
muscle and bone and sinew
borne on the animal wish;
Mother, the long generation
or the crest of the wave of the sea,
Mother, you have no notion
of what you have been or will be.

Round III

One wall slips from her world now
and she dances an open stage:
curtain up on painted flat.

          You may watch or dance along.

Card table center with folded table cloth.
Sideboard right. Phone. Clock. Teacups.
Window with the curtains drawn.

          Painting of the world beyond.

Toys scattered on the floor.
Coats. Shoes. Objet d'art.
Placed exactly as before.

          Fumbling at the door.

She searches for the keys.
At last it opens and she enters
madonna with bags and packages.

          Damn it! I forgot to get the flowers.

Because her days are all the same,
her feet move with the seconds,
now she is always counting hours.

          One o'clock!

High heels that click as she walks
across, across, back and forth,
moving her things, now all in the dance,

          (The garden club is coming.)

stage left, stage right, stage center.
Across, across, back and forth;
you may watch or dance along.

He: (His voice surrounding the stage.)
Mother, you are the flowers.
You are the fair mountain of flowers.
You are the banks of wild azalea.
You are the rise of blackberry roses.
You are the gentian and the columbine
and the high yellow flowers of the first of spring.
You are the deep red flowers of the tundra
and the blue and the white of the windblown crest.

She: Just two more hours.
All this to do by three!
(Reading a note on the telephone.)
"Call me at work as soon as you can."
What in the world does he think I am?

He: You are the earth and of it all the form.
You are the pod, the cone, the ear of corn.
You are the kernel of all that has been.
You are the seed of the world to come.

She: Darling, it's me. What do you want?

He: The sun and the moon and the stars
for all generations.

She: Till four. At five!

He: And the joy of the flesh and the earth
for those alive.

She: By six. Then seven.
(Kisses the receiver and hangs up.)

He: From the garden paradise
to the last explosion of the sun
I kiss you and I sing your praise.

(She pulls a deck of cards out of a bag.)

You are the deck of cards undealt.

(She pours herself a cup of tea.)

You are the shifting leaves of tea.
You are the teacup.
You are the deep and ever brimming sea.
You are the mother of all that has been,
of all that will ever be.

She: I am the mother. There we agree.
I am the spooner and the burper,
the wiper and the comber,
the scrubber of all elbows, ears and knees
and the one who cleans up after the puppy.
And no time now for your poetry!
I am the sewer, the mender,
the mixer, the blender,
the slave of your gleaming machines:
the toaster, the roaster,
the washer, the dryer,
the steam iron, the automobile.
Not what I want but what I have to be.
And shopping without stopping.
(Counting teacups.) Eight. Nine.
O damn it! Runs in my stocking.

He: You are the here and the now of time.

She: Ten. Eleven. Twelve.

Kicking off her high heels
she is out of the stage play,
back in the dance beyond.

She: I am. O!

Interlude III

With blue lotus feet and with stars in her hair
she is the dance and the dance is everywhere.
And everywhere she dances is music,
and everywhere music is motion,
and motion flows into matter,
and matter encompasses time.
And music and motion and matter
when she touches her fingers together
circle onward and outward forever.
  Chaos, creation and doom.
  Chaos, creation and doom.
  Chaos, creation and doom.

Round IV

The gravels that grind on the ocean bottom
have little to do with the moon
and now she is old and her flesh is unwinding
and soon with the tide she will drown
but with the momentum left to her
she dances another round.

Listen the old girl dancing
rattles her bones at the moon;
but listen, the moon is silent
and now she dances alone.

And all you can do however she dances
is patiently listen and watch.
Nor love, nor magic, nor pity, nor science
will lower the moon to her touch.

Rattling on and on—
living worlds now dead,
dreaming dreams of other dreams
sitting in a rocking chair
boxes inside boxes underneath her bed.

Rattling on and on—
Her once-upon-a-time is told,
and told and told again.
Have you heard about the circus?
Hoop snakes rolled by the light of the moon?
Of how I used to dance
round and around and round all night?

Rattling on and on—
Her happily-ever-after dream
has its end in a rattling dance,
a dance to a desolate satellite
with tides of stiffening pain.
A fall through a vortex boxes
deeper in and down.

Rattling on and on—
Her momentum slows to a wheel chair
that you must push around.
Feet that do not touch the floor.
Give me my things,
my watches and rings.
Deeper in and down.

Rattling on and on—
And all you can do however she dances
is patiently listen and watch.
Nor love, nor magic, nor pity, nor science
will lower the moon to her touch.

Rattling on and on—
Rattling through boxes,
deeper down and in,
rattling through boxes,
body, box and end.

Postlude

—and then the dance,
the singing movement,
the silver sound of stars rimming the sky,
of atoms universing by,
the rhythm wide, and wide and high—

Between the Shouting and the Toad

1958–1984

The Little Gods

The little god with a motor car
can skim the country near and far
and never need a north star.

The little god with a TV set
can watch the world and not regret
the death of a violet.

The little god with a radio
can listen wide and never know
the news about the rainbow.

But for their powers I have no need:
Once lost in a dark countryside
without my star to guide me

a violet about to die
took pity on my pain and told
me all about the rainbow.

Buddha and the Butterflies

The children run and shout at butterflies;
they trample flowers; they raise a frantic din;
but none they catch is even worth a pin
for if they hold one it is crushed and dies.

The toad who watches all with golden eyes
abruptly flicks one through his widest grin
alive, but as it folds to death within
he belches—disappointed at its size.

I sit between the shouting and the toad
midst butterflies pinpoint and eremite
and see their iridescene everywhere;
then motionlessly like a powerful lode
I draw the essence from their brittle flight—
then with them flicker in the breathless air.

The Ogre Garden

—and from those walls turn north to reach the heart
of town. Yes, that is where the ogre dwells.
You won't see him from the street; he's too smart.
Hardly! His garden grows too many hells:
Midst trees with leaves all clotted black are beds
of obscene lilies, tiger eyes, blue stemmed
passions thick with bile, oozing poppy heads.
He strolls about, his hairy arms begemmed,
and sniffs at these and plucks the virgin girls
who crouch in tubs of berries, rosy faced
with pleasant rash—whose lemon-flavored curls
roughen the palate to a luscious taste
    so sour I wish the earth would pucker her chin,
    purse tight her lips and suck this garden in.

Bathtub Botticelli

Curled in the tub she wonders at the red
so nicely placed, the smooth, textured patch,
the bubbling in the ancient maidenhead—
unaware there new ages wait to hatch;

then standing from the soap white suds that lave
her she is borne to waters, to blue thighs
where every age, with every kind of wave
the shallow shell shall from the seafoam rise.

So hail the virgin goddess of the sea
of life! Hail Mazie!—Venus here once more;
through her the world will always be with thee;
but pity her, for when she steps to shore
she'll hear, down through the vortex of the tub,
the leering gurgle of Beelzebub.

Socrates

Why seek old Socrates whose steps have passed,
whose circled friends have gone, whose hemlocked bone
sifts with the dust of all that Greece had massed:
He monkey-faced but for the nose alone?

"All men are mortal." This you dare to say
of him and yet proclaim his lust for truth,
philosophy that walks the streets by day
and love for giving life to teaching youth.

That truth he lived, which never since has died
(note well he never deigned to take up pen)
convinces me his daemons still abide
incarnate yet in wise and holy men.
    So when with luck I seek out one of these
    we meet again; in him is Socrates.

Sphinx

Often perplexed by Nature's strumpet ways,
her sky-wide smiles, her wild beckoning call,
the bloody darkness of her final jaws
I am tempted to snatch her florid veil
and dare expose her as she is: a jade,
a great sadistic mother with her spawn
held in her cruel paws: becuffed and clawed,
always alive, always dying in pain.

Yet though she is the sphinx, the monsterous slut,
she also is the chosen bride of God
and she if she does deem to feast on blood
will; O! but by accepting this our lot
together I, the tiger, and the dove
may from her breast here suckle her sweet love.

Apollo

Apollo dares to stroke his marble brow
and preen and sleek his white anatomy
as though he weren't immured, mere chipped debris,
in temples holy to the fig tree bough;

and though his tending priests do not allow
the show of any sensuality
he sways to pluck the shadow melody
which sculpture dared not freeze nor time endow.

So plug your ears—such rhapsody deflowers
the pure and pristine beauty cold as stone
and undulates and beats and overpowers
the bloodless chastity that won't condone
that Attic bodies once had hair like ours,
that classic lines were once by passion blown.

Clocks

How intricate the clock that ticks the time
approving every second of the day
and indicating minutes not to stray
until they've all been certified by chime.

In the same way in mighty pantomime
the swinging firmament the stars inlay
dividing portions days and years away;
but, Oh! how intricately more sublime.

And yet how smoothly do the ages flow
away from all we know so unconcerned
with any kind of clock's approving nod;
for Time has seen the stars above cut low
more times than all the clocks on earth have turned—
alone with the escapement hand of God.

Lotta Louise

Grandma keeps boxes underneath her bed!
boxes of boxes underneath her bed,
so many boxes you never get inside
telling of another world where everyone has died,
telling of another life a long time ago
of hoop-snakes and garter-snakes and Indians too!
and many, many things that she won't tell you.
Life was too sad then or life was too grand.

Grandma had big brothers who every Halloween
ran through the pumpkin fields—Oh you should have seen—
setting the outhouse where the bell had been
up on the school roof. And X-ing every barn.
My but they were bad boys and did such harm!
Stately old gentlemen in Sunday dress
to look at their photographs you never would have guessed.
And once when the circus came
the elephants got loose.
How? The grown-ups never knew,
and nobody to blame;
but Grandma will whisper how secretly to you.

She married Charlie Daugherty,
of whom we don't speak,
followed him to Kansas
for young love's sake.
Oh my! she's lived to rue that as her terrible mistake!

But when I ask about that
back in the boxes
mistakes are all laid by
and not even Mother will tell me why.

Song of the Earth

I have rocked the ocean cradle
    in my arms, in my arms;
I have rocked the brooding seas
    here in my arms
And since the sun first found me
I've held his warmth around thee
    so hush, so hush
I'll sing your hate away.

I have weaned the child of fury
    in my arms, in my arms;
I have weaned ungrateful man
    out from my arms
Yet when the moon has crowned me
I wrap my night around thee
    so hush, so hush
    I'll sing your hate away.

I will sing the cities quiet in my arms
    in my arms, in my arms;
I will sing all men to peace
    back in my arms
But till the stars confound me
I will with God surround thee
    so hush, so hush
    no more of hate today.

Poetry Reading

Poetry is magic:
a word becomes a jewel,
a string of words becomes a string of jewels:
diamond hitched to emerald,
emerald hitched to pearl,
rubies, topaz, amethyst
all on a golden chain.
Poetry is magic,
a chain of word and word,
an offering to a god
on some Olympus in the brain.

But yesterday when I brought my poems
to a group of restless teens
no god came—no magic—nothing:
nothing could take them from themselves,
from their adolescent pains.
The words all fell, all piled up on the floor.
And there with mud and chewing gum,
candy wrappers, tennis shoes and metal table feet
every word, every magic word mixed into the dirt.

Three years ago they would have heard the magic
and been enchanted children.
Three years from now when they have grown
and changed their pain for love
they'll be magicians on their own.
But yesterday the notes went back and forth:
I'll call at seven. Maurice is cute.
What do you say? Answer in the space below.
Why is that funny scarecrow standing there?
He should be at his computer or putting books away.
Mother Goose and William Blake—who are they?
Did the tiger kill Cock Robin? Who could care?
But let me know what you are going to wear
tonight when you answer the phone.

Blake gave emeralds to the tiger,
rubies to the cat,
but all he could give—for all they could take—
was a handful of dirt to each adolescent brat.

Actually some of them heard what I read from Nancy Willard's A VISIT TO WILLIAM BLAKE'S INN. Some of the best read aloud poems in a long time.

T'ien-Mu Mountain Ascended in a Dream

A seafaring visitor will talk about Japan,
which waters and mists conceal beyond approach;
but Yueh people talk about Heavenly Mother Mountain
still seen through its varying deepnesses of cloud.
In a straight line to heaven,
its summit enters heaven,
tops the five holy peaks,
and casts a giant shadow through China
with the hundred mile length of the Heavenly Terrace Range
which, just at this point, begins turning southeast.

My heart and my dreams are in Wu and Yueh.
And they cross mirror lake all night in the moon.
And the moon lights my shadow and me to the Yien River,
with the hermitage of Hsieh still there.
And the monkeys calling clearly over ripples of green water.
I wear his pegged boots up a ladder of blue cloud.
Sunny ocean halfway.
Holy cock crow in space.
Myriad peaks, more valleys and nowhere a road.
Flowers lure me, rocks ease me.
Day suddenly ends.

Bears, dragons, tempestuous on mountain and river
startle the forest and make the heights tremble.
Clouds darken with darkness of rain,
streams pale with pallor of mist:
the gods of thunder and lightning shatter the whole range.
The stone gate breaks asunder
venting in the pit of heaven an impenetrable shadow.

But now the sun and the moon illumine a gold
  and silver terrace,
and clad in rainbow garments, riding in the wind come
the queens of all the clouds
descending one by one with tigers for their lute players
and phoenixes for dancers.
Row upon row, like fields of hemp, range the fairy figures.

I move, my soul goes flying.
I wake with a long sigh.
My pillow and my matting are the lost clouds I was in.
And this is the way it always is with human joy:
ten thousand things flow forever like water toward the east.
And so I take my leave of you not knowing for how long.
But let me on my green slope raise a white deer
and ride to you Great Mountain when I have need of you.
Oh, how can I gravely bow and scrape
to men of high office and high rank
who will never suffer being shown an honest hearted face!

Chinese poem of the T'ang Dynasty by Li Po. This anonymous translation discovered while browsing bookstores in San Francisco's Chinatown in 1966. It is so vastly superior to other attributed translations that I don't want to take the chance of letting it get lost again. (The book was stolen from me and only the chance event that one of my students copied it has preserved it.) This, and because I love it are the reasons I want it printed with my poems.

PHOTO BY MATT GALLAGHER

Michael Conway is one of the personae of a man who lives in the west of Marin County. He taught school in that area for about 25 years. Subject integration being one of his strong commitments, he was innovative in many areas: math, art, literature, science, social studies, multi-media, writing, computers. He taught art to math students and math to art students and music appreciation to both. Some of his other personae are Mr. Conway (the teacher), Mike Conway (who is a gardener, friend and neighbor to many), and Myron J. Conway, Jr. (who signs the checks). One of his previous personae went to Dartmouth and got an MBA there.

Five hundred copies designed and produced
for the author at Archetype West by
Michael Sykes in the spring of 1985.
Printed and bound by Thomson-Shore, Inc.
Published by Floating Island Publications
from the Point Reyes peninsula
of Marin County, California.